DAYS WE WOULD
RATHER KNOW

Also by Michael Blumenthal
SYMPATHETIC MAGIC

DAYS WE WOULD RATHER KNOW

POEMS BY

MICHAEL BLUMENTHAL

THE VIKING PRESS

NEW YORK

First published in 1984 by The Viking Press
40 West 23rd Street, New York, N.Y. 10010

Published simultaneously in Canada by
Penguin Books Canada Limited

The author is deeply grateful to the staffs and directors of The
MacDowell Colony, The Ossabaw Island Foundation, The
Rockefeller Foundation, The Corporation of Yaddo, and the
D. C. Commission on the Arts & Humanities for their support
and for furnishing the uninterrupted time for the completion
and revision of this manuscript.

Library of Congress Cataloging in Publication Data
Blumenthal, Michael.
Days we would rather know.
I. Title.
PS3552.L849D3   1984   811'.54   83-40218
ISBN 0-670-77612-2

Pages 117–18 constitute a continuation of the copyright page.

Printed in the United States of America
Set in Baskerville

For Cynthia

Ah, Malte, we pass away like that, and it seems to me people are all distracted and preoccupied and pay no real attention when we pass away. As if a shooting star fell and no one saw it and no one had made a wish. Never forget to wish something for yourself, Malte. One should never give up wishing. I believe there is no fulfillment, but there are wishes that last a long time, all one's life, so that anyhow one could not wait for their fulfillment.

—RAINER MARIA RILKE,
Notebook of Malte Laurids Brigge

CONTENTS

I. SEASONS AND TRANSFORMATIONS

Night Baseball	3
The Elephants Dying	5
Dung Beetles	6
In a Helicopter over Parachute, Colorado	7
Looking for Wildflowers in Bernheim Forest	9
Mushroom Hunting in Late August: Peterborough, N.H.	10
Before a Storm, In September	12
October Sestina: The Shadows	13
Winter Light	15
The Earth Was Tepid and the Moon Was Dark	17
Christmas Eclogue: Washington, D.C.	18

II. BLUE

Blue	21
The Disappointments of Childhood	22
The Bluebird	23
The Old Painter at the Violin	25
Melancholy	27
Who Will Live in Our Houses When We Die?	28
Loss	30

Waving Good-Bye to My Father   31
The Bitter Truth   33
Learning by Doing   35
Juliek's Violin   36

III. ORDINARY/EXTRAORDINARY

Fish Fucking   41
Twice-Born Matches   44
The Snowstorm   45
Jungians & Freudians at the Joseph Campbell Lecture 47
Leap Child   48
A Man Lost by a River   49
The Angel Gabriel Is the Imagination   50
Watching La Bohème *with My Father*   51
A Photograph of Giacometti   53
Poem by Someone Else   54
The Litrajure of Everyday Life   56
Refinishing the Table   58
Ordinary/Extraordinary   59

IV. THE WOMAN INSIDE

The Woman Inside   63
Freudian Slip   65
Some Nights at Thirty   66
Couvade   67
Back from the Word-Processing Course,
    I Say to My Old Typewriter   69
Squid   71
The Music of Whatever   72

The Flirtation   73
Puer Aeternus   74
Weeding   75
The Garden   76
Poem, Against Hesitation   78
Last Supper   79
What Survives   80
In Assisi   81

V.   DAYS WE WOULD RATHER KNOW

Days We Would Rather Know   85
Wishes That Could Last a Lifetime   86
The Happy Poem   88
What I Believe   90
Young Birds Crying Late at Night   92
Praise   93
Today I Am Envying the Glorious Mexicans   95
This Is It   96
Over Ohio   98
I Am Sick of the Rich   99
Epithalamium: The Single Light   100
Drinks and Kisses   102
Light, At Thirty-Two   103
Father   105
The Cure   106
Wishful Thinking   108
The Puzzle   110
Cheers   112
Dayenu   114

Acknowledgments   116

I

SEASONS AND
TRANSFORMATIONS

Though trees turn bare and girls turn wives,
We shall afford our costly seasons;
There is a gentleness survives
That will outspeak and has its reasons.
There is a loveliness exists,
Preserves us, not for specialists.
                    —W. D. SNODGRASS,
                       "April Inventory"

NIGHT BASEBALL

[I] retrace by moonlight the roads where I used to play in the sun.
—MARCEL PROUST

At night, when I go out to the field
to listen to the birds sleep, the stars
hover like old umpires over the diamond,
and I think back upon the convergences
of bats and balls, of cowhide and the whacked
thumping of cork into its oiled pockets,
and I realize again that our lives pass
like the phased signals of that old coach,
the moon, passing over the pitcher's mound,
like the slowed stride of an aging shortstop
as he lopes over the infield or the stilled echo
of crowds in a wintered stadium. I see again
how all the old heroes have passed on to their
ranches and dealerships, that each new season
ushers in its crop of the promised and promising,
the highly touted and the sudden phenoms of the
unexpected, as if the hailed dispensation of gifts
had realigned itself into a new constellation,
as if the old passages of decrepitude and promise
had been altered into a new seeming. I remember
how once, sliding into second during a steal,
I watched the sun rest like a diadem against the
head of some spectator, and thought to myself
in the neat preutterance of all true feeling,
how even our thieveries, well-done, are blessed
with a certain luminousness, how a man rising
from a pilfered sanctity might still upright himself
and return, like Odysseus, to some plenitude
of feast and fidelity. It is why, even then, I loved
baseball: the fierce legitimacy of the neatly stolen,
the calm and illicit recklessness of the coaches

3

with their wet palms and arcane tongues of mimicry
and motion. It is why, even now, I steal away
from my wife's warm arms to watch the moon sail
like a well-hit fly over the stadium, then hump
my back high over the pitcher's mound and throw
that old curve of memory toward the plate
where I run for a swing at it—the moon
and the stars approving my middle-aged bravado,
that boy still rising from his theft to find the light.

THE ELEPHANTS DYING

If an elephant missteps and dies in an open place, the herd will not leave him there; the others will pick him up and carry the body from place to place, finally putting it down in some inexplicably suitable location. When elephants encounter the skeleton of an elephant out in the open, they methodically take up each of the bones and distribute them, in a ponderous ceremony, over neighboring acres.

—LEWIS THOMAS, *Lives of a Cell*

It is as if they are ashamed
of the body without its good visitor,
so when they come upon themselves,
more form than substance, more flesh
than the good ghost breathing, they'd
rather hide what's left of the empty hulk
than leave it to be found by us,
who might make jewelry of the tusk
and handbags of the floppy ears,
who might mistake the bones for clubs,
the silence for lack of testimony.

They'd rather die like their small brothers,
squirrels and the single-celled animals
who simply fade into each other like waves
near shore, noiseless and invisible.
They'd rather be remembered
for how the trunk swayed when the girls
still lived inside, for their bellyaching laugh
and how they beat the earth to sleep
with their huge feet, their tails,
their beautiful, dead bones.

DUNG BEETLES

They accept whatever excrement
life doles out to them gladly. Some
roll their balls along the grasslands
and savannas, excited as soccer players.
Others, concerned about the future, secrete
their hoards in the ground and wait for their spouses.
A third group, more like us, bury themselves
in their possessions until the dung breaks down,
exposing them for what they are.

It is a literal world, and a devious one:
When someone says to a friend, "Eat shit,"
he means it. And a man who buries his dung
deeply is sure to attract lovers—
swarms of them.

Even the singles bars are nothing more
than a pile of crap: a nuptial ball
where lonely beetles meet, shoot
the shit awhile, then flatten their dung
into the shape of a rug for dancing.

Finally,
flight-light and the earth unheaped,
they're off again—winging their way
toward the scent of some stooping elephant,
thanking the immaculate gods
for the divine orderliness
of this shit-ridden world.

IN A HELICOPTER
OVER PARACHUTE, COLORADO

I am not sure what the gods would have thought of this
or what, if they are still with us, they are thinking now,
but here above the rocked and ribbed and lovely planet,
I look down over the bruised elegy of mountains, over
the hacked landscape and mesmerized pastures of the elk
who once lived here, and I feel the strange restlessness
of my sad kind and their passion for dominion over the trees
and the birds and the relentless flowers. I feel the wide aura
of some otherworldly eye that looks down on this and wonders
what possible embellishment the torn and ravaged mesas
could bring to our lives, whether the blue columbine
and the magpie and the song of the meadowlark can survive
the good intentions of enlightened men and their lust for
improvement. Yesterday, walking beside a mountain stream,
I watched a single, speckled trout leap from the water,
flap its gills against the air, and pucker its mouth
like a child blowing kisses at an uncle he will never see again.
Alone there, I watched him slidder again into the glistening
stream, then disappear like song among the aspens and
wildflowers. A huge quiet came over the world then, as if
the gods themselves were holding their breaths in reverence
and wonder. And now I, no more or less a god than any man,
am flying over these streams and flattened peaks, my breath
held and my lips pressed like a child's face against the sky.
I see the vast carnage against the trees and the earth by those
I would like to call: *brother*. I see, or imagine I see,
that very trout fleeing like a wounded deer over the peaks,
glistening in the late afternoon light, and wondering if
its smooth course over the stones and silt and the penumbras
of flower will be swept to a cold end among the currents of
desire and progress. It must be wondering, I think,

how the soft underbelly of the earth can long survive
the metaled thrusts and pillages of cold steel we call future,
and why the sun and the earth and the clean undulations
of water do not suffice for our kind, and whether
the greatest kindness is not reverence, and whether men
can long continue to move mountains, or mountains men.

LOOKING FOR WILDFLOWERS
IN BERNHEIM FOREST

Louisville, Kentucky

The dogtooth violet, the chickweed
and the toothwort are all out,
the trees so neatly labeled
for the poets and forgetful.
We walk among these woods
(silent, fretful, full of doubt)
looking for loveliness others have named.

The horned owl undulates
its eyes within its cage;
the turkey vulture spreads
its wings but cannot fly.
The ring-necked pheasant's
mottled feathers mask its age;
the turtle bangs its head
against the glass and wonders why.

What's love? we ask ourselves
among these trees. *Whose
strange invention? What flowering
of shame?* As we continue walking
through the woods, calling out
such words as only love can name.

MUSHROOM HUNTING IN LATE AUGUST, PETERBOROUGH, N.H.

The drosophila wing of the morning moon
is still in the heavens
when, looking for the lesson in nature
we are always looking for, I walk,
basket in hand, through the damp woods,
parting the secretive ferns, twisting
my thin body among the asters and loosestrife,
checking beneath the stones and stumps
as I plunder the pine-needled floor
for the chanterelles and puffballs.

It is so much like life, which is why
I love it: the delectable and the deadly
so resembling each other, the sexual rise
of the false morel a mere flirtation,
and the sweet viscosity we'd like to swim in
an elegy to movement. Holding a knife
in my right hand, I work from the base,
cutting beneath the stipe, recording
in my small book the particulars
that separate delicacy from demise, hallucination
from the smaller contentments of mere vision.

Finally, placing each in its own small bag
and into my basket, I wend my way back
through the mossy woods to my soft chair,
to the embering fire where, with my book
and my magnifying glass, I start to separate,
because separating is, in the end, what this
is about: the doubtful from the certain,
the brief scintillations of beauty

from the urge for survival. Some, in fact,
are so beautiful I would like, this very moment,
to taste them: to feel the pale, red flesh
and feathery gills take on their sexual softness
beneath my tongue, but I am thinking again
of what a friend's psychiatrist said about women:
*"Just because they're beautiful and you're hungry,
doesn't mean you have to eat* all *of them."*

Until at last, what began as a large harvest
is merely a small bundle of certainty and safety.
And I sit there with my three piles of caps
and stems, of torn gills and the bruised flesh
of holiness and nature. Loving what little
I know for certain, I gather
the smallest pile toward me. *Oh life,*
I say to myself, *so this is what you are.*
I stumble out into the sunlight.
I pucker my lips at the morning moon.

And I eat.

BEFORE A STORM,
IN SEPTEMBER

Air inhales water and light so hard
it grows thick as placenta, and it seems

We are watching this life from another life,
embryos ourselves, and when the church bell

Strikes six, it is as if the heart of the world,
our mother, were beating a new rhythm,

As if all we had gathered together in times
of peace (beech, clover, song, dandelion)

Were breaking away from us, and our lives
were the fingers of a clenched fist, perfectly

Formed but inexperienced, a premonition
of what we are, ovarian form of a life we

Have not yet known, but are about to experience:
the opening of sky, then a quick flash of light,

The air surrendering its secret, and we
wet with the mere thought of it.

OCTOBER SESTINA:

THE SHADOWS

The maple that was amber this time
last night is now a ghostly shadow.
In fact, all that was beautiful
then is shadow, as if gods who once sang
were now whispering the names of the dead
and the world re-arranging itself beneath

the moonlight. The streets pass beneath
me, gold leaves fluttering one at a time
from the ginkgos like letters the dead
might send to a friend whose shadow
is passing above them, someone who sang
to them in times of loneliness. Beautiful

is not the word to describe the beauty
of this moment: sky and all that's beneath
it merging like smoke into smoke, a song
that's not just another homage to time,
but a fading of substance to shadow,
all that's alive mimicking all that's dead.

And yet—not discouraged by the deaths
that surround them—magnolias stay beautiful,
severe as eagles hovering in the shadows.
Leaves flutter like spawned salmon beneath
them. Who could believe that, time after time,
year after year, it continues, this song

of loneliness, repetition, a sanguine turning
and resurrection in which the live and the dead
are etched—each in his personal time—

like the irascible carvings of lovers beneath
the branches, and the light that was beautiful
only yesterday is darkness and widening shadow.

And yet the mockingbird sings in the shadows,
still the chrysanthemums hold to their unsung
resilience. And if nothing survives beneath
this winter's ice, if only the dead and their dead-
ening music are what's left of this beautiful
season, then who will remember this time, who

will remember these beautiful fallings, sing-
songing the quiet of this restless time, as the dead
spread their fingers beneath the widening shadows.

WINTER LIGHT

In the flat, clean light of winter,
the edges of monuments are smooth and precise
and all new significance gives way
to old significance. Perhaps it is only
the scent of old shirts reclaiming the body
that makes my mind drift with the first innuendos
of ice down the Potomac. Yet something insists
it's the light and—as I drive down this highway—
it is not the other travelers who are my brothers,
but the Andean condor, exceeding its habitat
and gliding over the forests.

Once, on a Caribbean island,
I found a rancid, foul-smelling fruit
among the bay leaves, broke it open on a stone,
and sucked its sweet pulp clean and delicious
with a vague relief. Now, here in a season
where nothing grows and days decline in light,
I think of my life as that fruit, of what a going in
there is in face of bad odors, unbeckoning anatomy.
I see the constant smallness of hands, how
all their turnings rebel at the intransigence of roads
and how regret is as senseless as anger
at weather . . . and weather is everywhere.

It must be the light: how it transforms
air to movement, breath to kindling,
how the drift of the mind rises to replace
what cold air falls. Perhaps it's the way
winter reminds us we are, finally, naked
under anything, or the persistence of pigeons,

for whom flight is the vehicle of return
and return the good order around all strangeness.

Look, again, at the monuments.
And think how stone rises toward light
for meaning, how the clean edge of things
thrives in darkness. And consider, perhaps,
how cold and the diminution of light combine
in your eyes, how your life might rise with
the coldness of stone and hover above everything,
in the stark, immaculate light of winter.

THE EARTH WAS TEPID AND
THE MOON WAS DARK

The earth was tepid and the moon was dark.
The children slept naked in their rooms
and feared the light. In the windy park
the leaves fell, and the crying of the loons
over the lake was all that foretold
the coming of winter and the brutal cold.

The night was quiet and the stars were bright.
The mollusks floated in the sea and paved the shore.
In the valley, within the gently misted light,
the cattle dreamt, and who could ask for more?
And in the pre-dawn hours of quiet sleep,
the dew lay glistening and the air was sweet.

Then the day dawned darkly and the birds awoke.
The church bells tolled. No one spoke
of love or death beneath the dimly lit trees,
amid the humming cars and the droning bees
that hovered and died against the brisk afternoon.
And then it was over, the day. And again the moon.

CHRISTMAS ECLOGUE:
WASHINGTON, D.C.

The homeless have all gone home
and the streets—quiet, abandoned—
belong again to those who find home
in the small movements of a day:
the whistling of kettles, the last fallings
of the ginkgo, the iambic drip-drop of rain
against windows. Not even ice has found
its way to our town this Christmas, and we
pause, suspended between seasons, the way
an old hiker pauses for breath before climbing.

And in this pause between things—
merriment and doom, the seventies and the eighties,
winter and the suggestion of winter,
things we pause between grow clear: ice,
loneliness, the meetings of glass and air
at windows. The whole world becomes a town
in which all leavings add to a vague clarity,
like the peacefulness of chessboards at checkmate
or the testimony of an empty stadium, all resonance.

Even this capital town—where lust and power
climb the trellises of the spirit like ivy—
knows, for a day, the peace of an empty room
in which all things have their place, but nothing
moves. Old couples rock at their windows
with the mute patience of monuments. Bluejays
welcome the morning without distinction.
Even the passage of ice eastward stops
in the Midwest for a day of prayer. Everything
that is not homeless pauses, looks around,
gives thanks, remains.

II

BLUE

And the color, the overcast blue
Of the air, in which the blue guitar

Is a form, described but difficult,
And I am merely a shadow hunched

Above the arrowy, still strings,
The maker of a thing yet to be made.

—WALLACE STEVENS,
"The Man with the Blue Guitar"

BLUE

the blue that will always be there as it is now . . .
—GEORGIA O'KEEFFE

Inside the hollowness that is bone
and the hollowness that is us, blue
is how it has always been and how
it will always be: the blue acres
of flesh we have traveled in search
of the propinquitous night, the blue
hours of morning before the mist rises
over the lake, the blue gaze of the sycamore
over the empty fields in February. Now,
it is dark and my bones open over the blue
sheets of the bed to welcome the night.
I gaze into the pale blue of your eyes
and see that I, too, am turning blue like
the graceful dead in their blue parlors
of silk and sweet dreaming. Last night,
the swallows prancing over the fields
were blue, and in the star-swift glide
of sky over the clouds, I realized
we end as we began, and moved along:
blue baby, blue sky, sweet blue grief,
the deep blue of no more breathing.
Tempera on paper or oil on canvas,
it is the blue envelope of the voice
that says *I love you,* and when the bones
open out into their pelvic dust, the blue
that is always blue is always there.

THE DISAPPOINTMENTS
OF CHILDHOOD

Perhaps a bird was singing and for it I felt a tiny affection, the same
size as a bird.

—JORGE LUIS BORGES

Imagine, now, an affection the same size
as the thing it's felt for—for the seed,
seedlike emoluments of liking, and,
for the rain, droplets of tenderness
clustered in small puddles at your feet.

And now remember how, as a child,
someone is telling you they love you.
How much does Daddy love you? they
ask, and you, childlike, spread
your arms as wide as a child can.

Little do you know it then, but
the rest of your life will be spent
measuring the distance between *"that* much"
and what love, in fact, is capable of—

the narrow width of a man or a woman,
their terrible thinness,
their small bones
growing constantly inward
from your spreading arms.

THE BLUEBIRD

Perhaps it was these signs of early spring
(the maple buds unfurling in the tepid air,
the crocuses extruding through the earth)

That lured this lovely, almost iridescent
creature north before its time this year,
and then again it may have been the sudden cold

(the icy winds unleashed against the trees)
that drove it frightened toward the chimney
of the house and downward through the flue.

How long it startled through this room, scavenging
what crumbs we may have left it late last fall,
battering the hapless curtains and the walls in vain,

We'll never know, though when we found it,
stiff and blue and breathless on the blue lake
of the rug, it seemed it couldn't have been long

At all since it had died its slow and silent death
right here, against the very spot where we
made love just months before. But death,

of course, is not what love's about, and though
the image comes to mind as I unbend my body
from the floor and hold the bird, its small legs

Arced like love into the vacant air, within my palm,
I know the noblest elegy for love is love itself,
that in the blue chambers of its stilled bird-heart

A candle of some other life than this is still aflame
as I, now opening the bedroom door to fling the bird
into the chilly, April night, still flame for you:

the spring that comes in earnest, even now.

THE OLD PAINTER
AT THE VIOLIN

in memory of Theo Fried, 1902–1980

Because it is his destiny
to love what is beautiful
and, what's more, to add to it,
he sits on his high stool,
before what he has already made,
in his jeans and blue sneakers
and his torn, gray socks,
and plays Vivaldi to his own Matisse,
Boccherini to his love for Cézanne.

On the easel before him,
in a white, luminous vase,
are the peonies and the poppies,
the dahlias and the bachelor buttons,
he has made from his mind's eye
the night before, and around him
his Bottom & Titania, and his dead wife,
who remains in this life and in the room
by his memory and by the rendering
that gives life to his memory.

"I went my own way," he says,
and so he goes, still. And so he goes,
as well, to his violin, not
to improve anymore, he admits,
but so as not to go backward,
because, even at seventy-eight, he says,
to go backward is the greatest sin of all.

And so he plays on. Not perfectly,
but beautiful just the same;
no better than yesterday, but

at least no worse. So that Vivaldi
and Cézanne would have been proud.
And as his arms glide over the strings,
he is a happy man: Happy
because he holds to his own vows,
happy because he never goes backward,
happy because the peonies and the violin,
in his hands, are one. Happy
because, in the cacophony of this life,
the one voice he always heard clearly
was his own.

MELANCHOLY

Though the flutist was beautiful,
you had forgotten you had never
liked woodwind quintets in the first place,
that the whole eighteenth century
seemed to you a bit like the loveliness
of azaleas in November.

You leave at intermission,
thinking of the tired arms of the Anasazi
as they carried water between kivas
of a vast pueblo, crying
their lovers' names from the mesa tops.

On the way home, you walk
through the park in a storm,
trying to capture your reflection
in the opaque leaves as they dance
among the turbulence of squirrels.

It is almost night
when the joys of this life
finally find you again,

Looking for tulips beneath the ice.

WHO WILL LIVE IN OUR HOUSES
WHEN WE DIE?

for Jody Bolz

In Bali, some friends were asked by a Balinese couple: "Do you
have any children?" When they replied that they didn't, the
woman then asked: "But who will live in your houses when you
die?"

The silent hush, the rusted hinges
creaking in the wind,
the emptiness of these closets
so ravenous for garments, who
would have thought our houses
would come to this? Years ago,
we sat here, in this large kitchen,
planning the lives of the unborn,
leafing through the pages
of Tolstoy and Chekhov for something
to name them. Now, wind leafs
through these rooms in search
of resistance, the old ghosts
of childhood sift the night, looking
for someone to frighten. Even
Rapunzel, old and emaciated, flings
the frayed rope of her hair
from the castle window, but no one
climbs it, and she dies a virgin.

Rising from the small, singular cots
of our celestial villages, we look down
on this: the mold mimicking grass
as it devours the ledges, the ivy
climbing like a pack of young boys
into the opaque windows, the willows
weeping and mopping their wet brows
against the shingles. Each year,

the earth is reclaiming more and more
of its progeny of sand; the heavens
reabsorb their tears from between
the bricks, the termites recycle
their mute homunculi of wood and ashes.
Silently, we look down on this,
and I turn to you:

Oh, friend, who will live in our houses
when we can no longer sleep in them? . . .

And how can the unborn sing for us
when we return to the earth?

LOSS

for David McAleavey

Something falls from you, life
or part-life, and you wonder
if, in the short orbit of breath,
there is an astronomy, or if the blood
of woman is the blood of ruin.

How do we sleep with all our impotence?
Imperviousness surrounds us, yet we
mimic urgency like jugglers or disco queens,
evangelists of our own significance.

I would rather believe the beautiful women
beneath the hair dryers. I would rather believe
the spouses contesting their small differences,
but loss persuades me: the children we father
who refuse to speak to us, the children we have
not yet fathered who will cry out at us in anger.

Loss persuades me it is real,
irrevocable,
unsure of its own resurrection.

As we are, David, as we are.

WAVING GOOD-BYE
TO MY FATHER

My father, folding toward the earth again, plays
his harmonica and waves his white handkerchief
as I drive off over the hills to reclaim my life.

Each time, I am sure it's the last,
but it's been this way now for twenty-five years:
my father waving and playing "Auf Wiedersehen,"
growing thin and blue as a late-summer iris,
while I, who have the heart for love but not
the voice for it, disappear into the day, wiping
the salt from my cheeks and thinking of women.
There is no frenzy like the frenzy of his happiness,
and frenzy, I know now, is never happiness:
only the loud, belated cacophony of a lost soul
having its last dance before it sleeps forever.

The truth, which always hurts, hurts now—
I have always wanted another father: one
who would sit quietly beneath the moonlight,
and in the clean, quiet emanations of some
essential manhood, speak to me of what,
a kind man myself, I wanted to hear.

But this is not a poem about self-pity:

As I drive off, a deep masculine quiet rises,
of its own accord, from beneath my shoes.
I turn to watch my father's white handkerchief
flutter, like an old Hasid's prayer shawl,

among the dark clouds and the trees. I disappear
into the clean, quiet resonance of my own life.

To live, dear father, *is to forgive.*
And I forgive.

THE BITTER TRUTH

The truth is a bitter truth—
Something I have wanted to say,
but am afraid, even now, to say:

That nothing excites me like excitement;
that love is rarely as exciting as the wish
for love; that the love of beauty is

A pagan toast at a Christian feast;
that the worship of beauty can destroy us,
because beauty is everywhere, and there

Are so few rewards for attention to it.
How can I tell you that you are beautiful?
And that she, too, is beautiful? *And she*

And she and she and it and he? How
can I tell you that the body I love
holds me prisoner despite my awe of it,

That I like to give of myself rarely
and in small quantities, that the pond
I go to drink from at dusk is sometimes

Full, sometimes empty, usually indifferent?
How can I tell you that, coming home
to find you in my bed, I am grateful

And indifferent both at once; that I have lied
because the truth is a bitter truth, an act
of complexity and confusion; because a lie

Is the one possible word before *good night*
and belief is only finding a lie we never
tire of; because to tell the truth is merely

To repeat the words *I do not know* until they
become insufferable; because to tell the truth
is to say hardly anything at all, and nothing

Delights like something said often and with
great conviction; because, if I tell the truth,
I too must end with *I do not know:* the sky,

the water on the lake, and the truth below.

LEARNING BY DOING

And now the day is mine and it is sweet.
I take this message from the light and make it real:
The loss we do not claim we must repeat.

Who knows if it is possible to cheat our fate?
In our denials, our wanting we reveal.
And the day is sometimes lost, and not so sweet.

A man can get through life—it's no great feat
To walk along the earth, or else to kneel.
But the loss he doesn't claim he must repeat.

Who lives alone, another doesn't cheat—
To wake alone at night and not to feel;
To call the day your own and make it sweet.

I've nothing more than words to seal my fate.
There's little that I want, still less I need.
So the loss I do not name I must repeat.

Who doesn't hate the unrelenting seed?
Who doesn't think his life's often unreal?
This day could be yours too, and could be sweet.
Just claim your loss tonight. And don't repeat.

JULIEK'S VIOLIN

Was it not dangerous, to allow your vigilance to fail, even for a moment, when any minute death could pounce upon you? I was thinking of this when I heard the sound of a violin, in this dark shed, where the dead were heaped on the living. What madman could be playing the violin here, at the brink of his own grave? It must have been Juliek. . . . The whole of his life was gliding on the strings—his lost hopes, his charred past, his extinguished future. He played as he would never play again.

—ELIE WIESEL, *Night*

Ahnest Du den Schöpfer, Welt? (World, do you feel the Maker near?)
—FRIEDRICH SCHILLER, "Ode to Joy"

In the dank halls of Buchenwald,
a man is playing his life.

It is only a fragment from Beethoven—
soft, melodic, ephemeral as the sleep
of butterflies, or the nightmares of
an infant, but tonight it is his life.

In one hand, he holds the instrument,
resonant with potential. In the other,
the fate of the instrument: hairs
of a young horse strung between wood,
as the skin of a lampshade is strung between wood.

Each note is a flicker of the lamp of his life,
and his father, an old conductor, listens
with the rapt attention of someone who knows
the finality of all moments, the power of music.

The bow glides over the strings, at first,
with the grace of a young girl brushing her hair.

Then, suddenly, Juliek leans forward
on his low stool. His knees quiver,
and the damp chamber fills with a voice
like the voice of a nightingale.

Outside, the last sliver of light weaves
through the fence. A blackbird preens
its feathers on the lawn, as if to the music,
and a young child watches from the yard,
naked and questioning.

But, like Schiller crying out—
Ahnest Du den Schöpfer, Welt?,
Juliek plays on.

And the children,
as if in answer,
burn.

III

ORDINARY/ EXTRAORDINARY

If you have three strings, you can eat.
—Geisha saying

FISH FUCKING

This is not a poem about sex, or even
   about fish or the genitals of fish,
So if you are a fisherman or someone interested
   primarily in sex, this would be as good a time
As any to put another worm on your hook
   or find a poem that is really about fucking.

This, rather, is a poem about language,
   and about the connections between mind and ear
And the strange way a day makes its tenuous
   progress from almost anywhere.

Which is why I've decided to begin with the idea
   of fish fucking (not literally, mind you,
But the *idea* of fish fucking), because the other
   day, and a beautiful day it was, in Virginia
The woman I was with, commenting on the time
   between the stocking of a pond and the

First day of fishing season, asked me if this
   was perhaps because of the frequency with which
Fish fuck, and—though I myself know nothing at all
   about the fucking of fish—indeed, I believe

From the little biology I know that fish do not
   fuck at all as we know it, but rather the male
Deposits his sperm on the larvae, which the female,
   in turn, has deposited—yet the question
Somehow suggested itself to my mind as the starting
   point of the day, and from the idea of fish

Fucking came thoughts of the time that passes
    between things and our experience of them,
Not only between the stocking of the pond and our
    being permitted to fish in it, but the time,

For example, that passes between the bouncing
    of light on the pond and our perception of the
Pond, or between the time I say the word *jujungawop*
    and the moment that word bounces against your
Eardrum and the moment a bit further on when the
    nerves that run from the eardrum to the brain

Inform you that you do not, in fact, know
    the meaning of the word *jujungawop,* but this,
Perhaps, is moving a bit too far from the idea of
    fish fucking and how beautifully blue the pond was

That morning and how, lying among the reeds atop
    the dam and listening to the water run under it,
The thought occurred to me how the germ of an idea
    has little to do with the idea itself, and how
It is rather a small leap from fish fucking to the
    anthropomorphic forms in a Miró painting,

Or the way certain women, when they make love,
    pucker their lips and gurgle like fish, and how
This all points out how dangerous it is for a
    man or a woman who wants a poet's attention

To bring up an idea, even so ludicrous and
    biologically ungrounded a one as fish fucking,
Because the next thing she knows the mind is taking
    off over the dam from her beautiful face, off
Over the hills of Virginia, perhaps as far as Guatemala
    and the black bass that live in Lake Atitlán who

Feast on the flightless grebe, which is not merely
    a sexual thought or a fishy one, but a thought

About the cruelty that underlies even great beauty,
　　the cruelty of nature and love and our lives which

We cannot do without and without which even the idea
　　of fish fucking would be ordinary and no larger than
Itself, but to return now to that particular day, and to
　　the idea of love, which inevitably arises from the
Thought that even so seemingly unintelligent a creature
　　as a fish could hold his loved one, naked in the water,

And say to her, softly, *Liebes, mein Liebes;* it was
　　indeed a beautiful day, the kind filled with anticipation
And longing for the small perfections usually found only
　　in poems; the breeze was slight enough just to brush

A few of her hairs gently over one eye, the air was
　　the scent of bayberry and pine as if the gods were
Burning incense in some heavenly living room, and
　　as we lay among the reeds, our faces skyward,
The sun fondling our cheeks, it was as if each
　　time we looked away from the world it took

On again a precise yet general luminescence when we
　　returned to it, a clarity equally convincing as pain
But more pleasing to the senses, and though it was not
　　such a moment of perfection as Keats or Hamsun

Speak of and for the sake of which we can go on for
　　years almost blissful in our joylessness, it was
A day when at least the possibility of such a thing
　　seemed possible: the deer tracks suggesting that
Deer do, indeed, come to the edge of the woods to feed
　　at dusk, and the idea of fish fucking suggesting

A world so beautiful, so divine in its generosity
　　that even the fish make love, even the fish live
Happily ever after, chasing each other, lustful
　　as stars through the constantly breaking water.

TWICE-BORN MATCHES

And as it should be with a true poet,
He puts the burned matches
Back into the box.

—YEHUDA AMICHAI

I sit by the water, a box
of burned matches in my pocket.
My shadow drinks from the waves
as they wash ashore, my body
feeds on the seaweed and dead fish
that lie beside me.

Suddenly,
a large black man
emerges from the ocean and walks
toward me. He is the man I have
been dreaming of for years, the man
who stands beside the dead bodies
of my family, without flinching,
and drinks from the blood that remains
in their veins. He is the man who is
always quiet amid my turbulence.

He walks from the water,
holding a damp cigarette between his lips,
and stands beside me. He asks me
for a light. Part fear, part courage,
I reach into my pocket for my matches,
hoping to find one
that will burn a second time.

THE SNOWSTORM

White's the crazed color of the day
and, from its first-built cell, the soul
uddles out toward some cool Connecticut,
before the dark drippings of the dogs and while
the storm's still on, carried by none of the networks
in its brief, transmogrifying, homogenizing splendor,
streaking and strumming and straining the air,
bending the bows and bowing our heads
to its sweet tickle against the eyes, driving
the driven to their feet and the infirm inside,
raising the cold equity of the shovels and urging
a calm and persistent horniness toward the scrotum
as we glide, waxed skis hissing like a wet beach,
beneath the railroad trestle and toward the canal.
What a day!—The quilled and chiaroscuroed trees
overhanging the river; the pointillist sheet of the canal,
as in an all-white Pissarro, even the starved starlings
seeming to caw in quatrains. And then,
as if to remind us that loss can be found anywhere,
etched in white chalk on the gray wall of the tunnel:
MARY LOVES KEN BUT KATHY WON, MAY 12, 1979,
but we ski by it, laughing at Mary's folly, which
someday may again be ours, because today's not the day
for loss, but for whiteness, for the blanched innocence
of snow and neighborliness and the halted frenzy
of getting anywhere, because we know that morning
will bring again the botched resurgence of disquietude:
the gray, graying and gruesome exhaust and unlent shovels,
the slushed disillusionments of the Marys and Kens.
But it is enough merely to have seen the earth as it was
this day: so white, so lovely, so bleached of small hatreds

and infinite partings that even the dead, this day,
must have turned white in their white beds, that—
when the gray, ordinary, expectable morning returns—
all who wake to it will have seen the earth, at least once,
as a porcelain of white stillness, a thing of such beauty
that all our illusions of mastery could turn white
and we could pause for a moment merely to gaze at it,
to praise the day and relish the pure, momentary
whiteness of our lives before moving on once again
into the real and quotidian darkness of the next afternoon.

JUNGIANS & FREUDIANS
AT THE JOSEPH CAMPBELL LECTURE

The Jungians are all wearing purple
and are fat, believers
in the archetypal pancake. The Freudians
wear dark gray and are thin
from all their *Lieben und Arbeiten.*
Phallic and yonic is how the afternoon goes,
myth and icon, serpent and mother earth.
And if Dali's drooped clocks are merely
a joke about time, for the Freudians
there's a menopausal tinge to that sagging hour.
And if the serpent in the grass is just
another word for love, to the Jungians
there's a rebirth waiting in the slipped skin,
a worm in the apple.

But in the end, it's all in good fun,
and everyone leaves happy—
The Jungians crying Freudian tears
into their lavender garments,
the Freudians purple with laughter
in their dark gray suits,
everyone delighted and friendly
over Jungian wine and Freudian doughnuts
in the pale, white room.

LEAP CHILD

for Howard Nemerov, 2/29/20

Born on a day which comes again
but does not come again each year,
he grows old and younger both at once:
Chronology's the music, yet his is
the off-beat of calendar's asymmetry,
jazz step in an otherwise classical tune,
so he measures himself against both
our time and his own, counting four
for every one of ours, one for every four.

And if the year skips like a scratched record
at the thought of his birth, it bothers him not:
He goes on graying at the temples either way.
And when February's ice gives way to March,
he waits at the border, counting himself blessed
to have been born at all, though the stuttering
years sometimes skip over his good name
without even calling.

A MAN LOST BY A RIVER

There is a voice inside the body.

There is a voice and a music,
a throbbing, four-chambered pear
that wants to be heard, that sits
alone by the river with its mandolin
and its torn coat, and sings
for whomever will listen
a song that no one wants to hear.

But sometimes, lost
on his way to somewhere significant,
a man in a long coat, carrying
a briefcase, wanders into the forest.

He hears the voice and the mandolin,
he sees the thrush and the dandelion,
and he feels the mist rise over the river.

And his life is never the same,
for this having been lost—
for having strayed
from the path of his routine,
for no good reason.

THE ANGEL GABRIEL IS
THE IMAGINATION

in memory of Wallace Stevens

He did not know if madness would survive into the night,
    Or if he would turn in his sleep to turn again

And all would be mere residue of what it was,
    A gimmick of itself that neither rises nor endures

In the oligarchic reign that was his democratic way.
    He knew that what he knew was not the sum of what he knew,

And what he didn't know the measure of exactly who he was.
    He knew the empty plate for the feasts it held,

And the rich harvest for its unrelenting famine.
    He knew the empty shell for the echo of the crab,

And heard the heels on pavements for what they were:
    The congealed ticks and tocks of our separate ways.

And he knew we all go mad no less than twice to be redeemed.
    And this is how he was, and this is how he woke:

With hardly a ripple in his sea that wasn't smooth,
    With hardly a tear in his old coat that didn't reek of divinity,

With never a hand in his deep pockets that came up empty.

WATCHING LA BOHÈME
WITH MY FATHER

I used to wonder why these simple deaths
would take so long: the large soprano
playing Tosca pausing for a breath
as she ascends the parapet, the piano
echoing her Mario's farewell. How dull,
I thought, this dying—Rigoletto's crying

And long shaking of his fists at the mute heavens,
so long until Don Carlo wounds his sister's heart
in *La Forza del Destino.* When I was seven,
while at *Carmen,* I recall how, by the part
when Don José pounds out his broken cry ("O
Carmen! Carmen!"), I thought no one would die.

But now, ourselves like two old tenors,
we sit here, watching Mimi serenade
Rodolfo, and I understand at last the tremors
of our long singing, and its purpose. I don't degrade
these long and lush librettos of dénouement anymore—
I sit here, awed, as Mimi drags herself across the floor.

And I reflect upon the long and painful arias
of our duet, its strange and ancient repertoire,
reverberant with rotten human bonds and barriers.
Oh, father, here we sit at last, in her boudoir,
convinced the loveliness of song expels its sadness,
that even tragedy, well sung, reveals a gladness

In the unextinguished heart. And so at last
we learn to love like this: the cindered past

merely a prologue to our long cantata,
the arias all sung, our dying's imprimata.
For we have learned to sing together rather well—
before the lights went out, before the curtains fell.

A PHOTOGRAPH OF GIACOMETTI

after Cartier-Bresson

The man's life is his work,
and so his body, in life,
is the body of a man crossing
a rainy street in Montparnasse:
his coat drawn, cowl-like,
over his angular head as he walks
a line of dots leading
from this life to the next.

He is so thin, so perfectly thin,
that between the two trees
that frame him as he crosses
the street, he is a third tree—
a line crossing a line between lines.

Even now, as he crosses the rain-
swept street, he is already the ghost
of himself he has always been making:
a long shadow crossing the glazed street
to reclaim his body, before the rain does.

POEM BY SOMEONE ELSE

This is not my poem
but a translation
of a poem
by a foreign poet
much admired
in my country.

It is a poem
of simple language:
stone, body, blood and flower,
and of simple events:
of being born
and being certain
to die,
of making love
to one woman
in the name of all women,
and of gathering each night
the bits of dust
that fall from us
and pouring them back
into the body,
so that the next day
might begin again.

This is not my poem,
but a poem which—
if I were a citizen
of another country—
I would write for you.
And you would love it,

I'm absolutely certain.
So I have translated it
from the Czech and the Hebrew
and the Polish and the Italian
of the poets I admire.
So you can feel free
to love it. Since
it is not my poem,
but only my brother's—

who lives in another country.

THE LITRAJURE OF
EVERYDAY LIFE

for Anthony and Helen Hecht

Nothing derivative here:
just the breezed pancake
of afternoon, the wafted entrails

Of the scarves blowing in iced air
and the girls, Ah the girls, not a single one
out of an Ingres painting, not a single one

Brushing her hair as in Renoir,
but lovely still among the splotched
particulars of an ordinary afternoon,

Among the dark and dandy and fanciful
trees, so ravenous to be leafed
and still stippled in their shading.

What a day! The sweet frottage of afternoon,
not really as in a Max Ernst painting,
but still chalked and textured and

Chiaroscuro-like in its deep vintage
of blue-gray, the high strut
of the terribly busy, and the pursed lips

Of girls in the library, bookish
only to seem reticent, but eager still
to indenture the evening

Between the high lubricants of lust
and tenderness, the straggled juices
that flow all over this horny world

Like the Three-in-One Oil of some
creaked Divinity, the so-glad-to-
know-you-but-let's-get-on-with-it

Of easy access, and now already
the bagels are plopping like galoshes
from their back-room ovens, the pizzas

Are sizzling beneath their cheeses
and the world is a pretty place, mixed
in media and nonreferential, a patchwork

Of intent and coincidence, a sweet *res ipsa*
of things found and stumbled upon, as this
was stumbled upon, bright and ordinary

And unmediated from within the sweet
potpourri of its ribbed compendium:
nowhere indexed, nowhere to be found in books.

REFINISHING THE TABLE

You still remember the nick your sister made
with her spoon, and when we come to it,
beneath the old varnish and time-settled stains
of use and misuse, you say so, as if to remind me
that the small momentos of hurt and repair
are all we are left with. But we begin, elbow
to elbow, the way lovers left in a familiar sleep
learn to love one another, until what once was
surface is surface again, a deep pentimento
you ate from and now would feast at once more.
O love, this is our life: this rubbing and rubbing
at the dim, artificial gloss the heart's veneered with,
this deep retrieval. And here we are: a man
and a woman who give life and who take it away,
elbow to elbow in the late afternoon, breathing
the breath of our arms into the half-dead wood,
calling your sister, the dead trees and the
mute children of another life back to the table.

ORDINARY/EXTRAORDINARY

for May Stevens

Courage and sleep, Lindsay said,
are the principal things. And so
our mothers sleep, and our heroes,
who sleep too, are sometimes courageous.

The other day I saw you
among the extraordinary wildflowers,
a woman whose ordinary mother,
like all our mothers, startled each day
away from words we try and startle to.
I saw you there, outside the clear,
rectangular wishing wells of my window,
your black hair dittoing the black-eyed Susans,
your arms scissoring among the ferns and butterflies.

It was as if you wanted,
by being in nature, to be part of it.
But we, we ordinary sleepers, are never
part of it: We merely visit there
in small bursts of courage our sleep allows.
We take the large, cumbersome pieces
of our interior lives, the rockers
and stuffed armchairs, and carry them out
among the ferns and sunlight, before
returning again to sleep in the dark rooms
of our speechlessness and terrible timidity.

You were all metaphor there,
in the beautiful light: Our lives
are the extraordinary flowers
we carry, speechlessly,
into our ordinary rooms.

IV

THE WOMAN
INSIDE

In the Woman is the seed of the Man,
In the Man is the seed of the Woman,
Throughout all time, one lives within the other,
All longing is their need to re-unite,
All seeking is their striving to repair
The wound of separation long ago,
All joy is the joy of each to find the other.
                    —MARY KIMBALL, "The Web"

I am the poet of the woman the same as the man,
And I say it is as great to be a woman as to be a man,
And I say there is nothing greater than the mother of men.
                    —WALT WHITMAN, "Song of Myself"

THE WOMAN

INSIDE

There is a woman
inside me.
She is not beautiful
or divine,
but when I turn
in my sleep, restless
with other worlds,
she is always there—
placing a lilac
in my hand, gesturing
to the earth where
it all begins and
all ends. She knows
there are cruel men
everywhere, and angels
in unlikely places.
She knows the darkness
is only a passage
between light and light,
that the wisteria
climbing the house
are real, and lust
only tenderness gone wild
in the wrong field.
She is the one who is
always fertile in times
of barrenness, the one
with the silver hair
carrying a candle
through the long tunnel.
She is Halcyone,

calming the waters
after all my deaths;
she is Eurydice,
refusing to fade
when I look behind me.
She is the one
who wakes
with her arms around me
when I wake
alone.

FREUDIAN SLIP

Though she coaxes the embroidered silk
over her head with the care of someone
attending a ball, the slip is transparent,
and in the moonlight filtering through
the bedroom window, her body is even
more real for its inspired accidents:
her breasts brazen and shy both at once,
mangos and the ordinary flesh.

It is how mistrust begins: this
and the second voice that whispers
beside you while she sleeps, the thrush
with a bluejay's cadence, archipelago
with its islands strung together so tightly
it mimics the mainland. And when she says
night, love, night frightens me, you know
she does not mean darkness.

And when she says *I love you,*
she means *watch your step,*
the rest of your life.

SOME NIGHTS AT THIRTY

Some nights you are the dirty girl from Iowa
who said *oh baby it hurts so good.*

Some nights you are the twelve-year-old
in the Danskin ad with no hair anywhere.

Some nights you are the wild virgin
who's done everything but for fifteen years.

Some nights you are the Dutch girl in the park
whose only English was *oh* and then *oh oh oh*
and then *oh* again.

Some nights you are the woman I worked with
who said, every day at noon, *let's do it here, now,
the hell with decency.*

Some nights you are all the beautiful women
in Copenhagen and I am a bicycle seat.

Some nights you are the whore at the Mustang
Guest Ranch, telling me I'm your twenty-third trick,
saying *you young kids all want somethin' for nothin'.*

Some nights you are the wild blonde who rides horses
naked in the moonlight and makes love in the kitchen.

Some nights you are the girl in the mental hospital elevator
who said: *hey, mister, you're cute, wanna wrestle?*

And some nights, thirty and tired of sleeping
with strangers, you are only yourself: calling me
Bruce, John, Rachel, Daddy, telling me *giddy-up,*
shifting me to first gear and pedaling like crazy,
in our old bed of fantasy and remarkable absences.

COUVADE

for H.

When your wife uttered your son
like a large syllable into this world,

you, ever the generous one, took sick too.
You took to bed and, in the large,

violent strokes that heaved beneath your belly,
it was as if you were a woman—as if by

the mere ache and purgation of your wounds
you could return to the place we have all

been exiled from; as if, by mimicking
the motions of your own child's mother,

you could be, to them and to yourself,
all things: child, father, a man so womanly

in his own being that he could, somehow,
bear his own child into the world with his wife

like a duet. It was so kind of you. And I
imagine she, too, must have known it:

How a man aches at times like these toward
places he has left and can never return to;

how he looks into the faces of his own wife
and child and staggers to bed in the sheer

empathy and pain of wanting to become them.
And how, when his wife rises from the dimmed

light of their child's afterbirth, he too
will rise, and all that is good in this world

will speak his name into the tight tercet
of their togetherness. And his son
will call him Father, and his wife: a man.

BACK FROM
THE WORD-PROCESSING COURSE, I SAY
TO MY OLD TYPEWRITER

Old friend, you
who were once in the avant-garde,
you of the thick cord
and the battered plug,
the slow and deliberate characters
proportionally spaced, shall we
go on together as before?
Shall we remain married
out of the cold dittos of conviction
and habit? Or should we move on
to some new technology of ease
and embellishment—Should I run off
with her, so much like you when
you were young, my aged Puella
of the battered keys, so lovely
in that bleached light of the first morning?

Old horse,
what will it be like
when the next young filly
comes along? How will I love you,
crate of my practiced strokes,
when she cries out: *new new*
and asks me to dance again?
Oh plow for now, old boat,
through these familiar waters,
make the tides come in
once more! Concubined love,
take me again into your easy arms,

make this page wild once more
like a lustful sheet! Be wet,
sweet toy, with your old ink:
vibrate those aging hips again
beneath these trembling hands.

SQUID

So this is love:

How you grimace at the sight
of these fish; how I pull
(forefinger, then thumb)
the fins and tails from the heads,
slice the tentacles from the accusing eyes.

And then how I pile the silvery ink sacs
into the sieve like old fillings, heap
the entrails and eyes on a towel in the corner;
and how you sauté the onions and garlic,
how they turn soft and transparent, lovely
in their own way, and how you turn to me
and say, simply, *isn't this fun, isn't it?*

And something tells me this all has to do
with love, perhaps even more than lust
or happiness have to do with love:
How the fins slip easily from the tails,
how I peel the membranes from the fins
and cones like a man peeling his body
from a woman after love, how these
ugly squid diminish in grotesqueness
and all nausea reduces, finally, to a hunger
for what is naked and approachable,

tangible and delicious.

THE MUSIC OF WHATEVER

The way Goethe counted out hexameters
on his Roman lady's back, I count

the unkissed syllables the wind wafts over
the grasses and horse farms of Kentucky,

I count the dark pentameters of fallen leaves
that the soft rains of April will transform

to the mulch of a new season. O love, this
is what we are here for—to make music

of both presence and absence, to sing
whatever song first comes to us over the dark

parapets of decay and distance, to emulate
the greased happiness of the mallards floating

among the pond scum and incipient flowers.
It is why I count out the beat of whatever song

first comes to me amid our half-ruined lives,
and why what I count, in whatever form

the angels find for it, becomes the measure
of some new and intoxicated holiness: the buds

on these barren trees yearning to flower,
your voice in the unchilled wind making music

of *even this even now even here.*

THE FLIRTATION

I am tired of looking at you through this glass.

Up close, I'm sure your eyes are a deeper green,
your hair the scent of Vermont in September.
I am sure we are in total agreement about the
importance of milkweed, the intrusiveness of money.

I see you cruising the ferns and coffee tables
of this building, eyes beating your forehead for a
glimpse of me, your legs a chorus of violins.
You must know I am not really up here working,
but am holding you like a key to the threatening sky.

I watch you wash other men's hair, your fingers
dancing like ribbons around their temples.
Your breath fills them with foolish suggestions,
makes me want to curl my own hairs around you,
discuss the justice of distances.

At night, two high-priced whores,
we go home to strangers, make love
in satin sheets, sipping imported brandy:
whispering each other's name to the impossible windows.

PUER AETERNUS

Le Poète est semblable au Prince des Nuées
Qui hant la tempête et se rit de l'archer;
Exilé sur le sol au milieu des huées,
Ses ailes de géant l'empêchent de marcher.

—CHARLES PIERRE BAUDELAIRE,
"The Albatross"

The wax wings of Icarus haunt you
as you fly upward calling *not here,*
not here, pure youth that you are,
celestial dreamer, vagabond
of everywhere. Where you've been
this night is no home for tomorrow:
no shape grows firm around your body,
the waters you swim in too restless for ice.

But somewhere someone imagines you quiet:
A Senex silently burns for you in the shadows,
holding her cold rope and her flame
beneath your wings as you rise from the water.
Pure darkness, she could be yours forever—
a side of yourself you loathe so well you'll
marry it, make it your victim and lover.

But, somewhere, a friend calls out to you
from the shadows: The kind voice of Daedalus
whispers its warning as you head for the sun.

WEEDING

Some say it's woman's work, this bending
and kneeling toward the earth, this task
that separates what feeds from what is fed,
and if it is then I am woman now, pulling
the green from the green, sifting the dirt,
praising the sweet conspiracy that has made
leaf of the seed, and work of my idleness.

Once, I loved a woman who held
the scent of dirt like perfume in her hands,
whose very voice could make the seeds grow
in any weather. Now, I am becoming
that woman, so that the next one I love
need be nothing I have yet a name for.
And someday, I believe, the earth's good works
will belong to anyone, a sweet dream
without gender or contentiousness in which
all who bend with a good heart toward what
survives can be called: *mother.*

Loving a woman now
who makes me man, immune
to any task the mind can simplify,
I bend my body, lovely in its ribs,
toward the earth again, so that the man
and the woman who live inside it may find
peace together, so that all that is separate
inside my life might finally sing: the one song
I have been practicing all these years,
in any place the gods might pause to occupy,
as they do here and now, Amen.

THE GARDEN

It is an old story, older
than the sweet psychiatrists
with their fifty-minute hours, older
than the beatific gardens and live oaks
and palmetto fronds that sway
beside the salt marshes of Ossabaw,
older even than the stolen birthright
and blessings of Esau and the backward glances
of Orpheus and Lot's wife, with their lost loves
and pillars of salt.

It is the story of the restlessness of the soul
inside the body, and of the anger of the body
at the soul's infidelity. It is the story
of edifice and orifice, of Orpheus and Eurydice,
and of the sweet completion we all yearn for
and strive against like moths whose deaths
gleam in the same light that saves them.

Now, I am once again living in the darkness
of my own confusion, a man
who loves women and the parched earth
and his thirst for water. All that completes me
tears at the fragile seams of seeming calm.
All that offers warmth offers fire, and we
who slept together in the womb of another time
now wake as rivals in a sea without estuaries.

To make love to any woman, he said, *is to
tamper with fate.* And if it's true, perhaps
I have twisted the soft wings of destiny

to a place of no shape and no movement,
perhaps I have driven the sweet waters
from my own shore in search of treasure,
only to find the earth parched and my tongue
dry with a thirst for moisture and sanctity.

Mother and brother, sister, lover, husband,
daughter, infidel and father. The stage fills
with a cast thrown into a play written for harlequins.
Out of a single torso, the hydra-headed monster
rises and walks to center stage, and though
we bury its immortal head beneath a stone,
though we sear the open necks of its severed heads
to clear the air, they sprout again, leaving us
calling out into the crowd for someone to save us.

Now, there is a sleep and a mist, a sleep and a mist
and the love-lust of a strange and bitter time.
Only the wild dogs and dream-icons remember
what it was to love. But there are a man and woman,
and they want to love each other, but have fallen
into the deep reveries of the hydra-headed self.
There is a dream that requires sleep to find its meaning.
There is a man and there is a woman and their arms
are locked around each other in a deep sleep aimed
at finding who they are, at finding who they will be,
in the new garden from which all eat,
and in which no one wants to plant.

POEM,

AGAINST HESITATION

Her tilted chin mimics the rise
of a swallow from seaweed to juniper,
and her lemon hair against the fresh-
cut grass is mustard to your basil.

She has drunk the wine you planted
beside her, sucked the pulp from
the tangerine, and pitted the grapes
with the foreskin of her delicate tongue.

Soon the sun will retreat behind the maple,
the mockingbird will have bored of its repertoire,
and the light her eyes now gleam in will light
a funeral in Singapore or a circumcision in the Negev.

Oh, kiss her already, you fool,
the darkness surrounds us.

LAST SUPPER

None of us is Christ, really,
or even a hero, yet, in the
luminescence these candles lend to
our faces, it could be that every man
and every woman is a hero.

And it may be, as the light flickers
first to your face, then to mine,
that when the blood cools and a man
is left with only other men, whispering

To music over a meal still warm with
a woman's certainty, truth finds its way
easily, like the telling of an old war story
or a boat heaving in the waters of Asia,
rich and frightening without embellishment.

And it becomes, finally, a question
of why, and to what purpose, we live at odds
with what we need, like a sentence running
mercilessly over its own meaning. Perhaps

The answer suggests itself in the dripping
of wax down this old candelabrum: that we
are a burning that diminishes itself
by the light it gives others, men letting
their best testimony run like wax down

The thighs of a stranger, until we betray
the hero that lives inside us, and night
descends over three men fingering the truth
of themselves in the solitary darkness:
the wax of their spent lives.

WHAT SURVIVES

Over the dulling years,
you write poems for hundreds of women—
about love, the impossibility of love,
the way light bounces off the edge
of a table. Those survive best—
the ones about light, that is.

Very few write back.
It's like a long correspondence
with an autistic child: Every cry's
a cause for ecstasy. The ones who do
always say something about Chopin:
How it is difficult to sleep to his music,
how the dance of your tongue to his nocturnes
seem insincere.

It could go on like this forever.
You develop theories about Jungian typology,
the specialized function of the sides of the brain.
You begin looking at furniture as if it mattered.
You reflect upon the multiple meanings of silence.

There's one consolation—
You know all this must be teaching you something.
About love.
About language.

About the light on the table.

IN ASSISI

This morning, in Assisi, I woke
and looked into my wife's face
and thought of Saint Francis:
how he explained to Brother Leo
that Perfect Joy is only on the Cross,
how he told him that, if they should come
to the Convent of Saint Mary of the Angels,
soaked with rain and frozen by the cold
and soiled with mud and suffering
from hunger, and if they should knock
on the gates and a porter should come out
and beat them over the head with a knotty club
and throw them down into the mud and snow
and cover their bodies with wounds, only then
might they know Perfect Joy. And I thought
of how Saint Anthony converted the heretics
by talking to the fishes, and of how blood flowed
from a picture of Saint Francis's stigmata,
and of the beautiful death of Brother Bernard.
And I looked again into my wife's lovely eyes,
both green and grey at once in the Umbrian light,
and swore to myself, rolling over beside her,
that I would never be a man who flings his body
like dirt against the thorns, that I would never
lie down to sleep on a bed of stone; that,
if I were ever fit to preach to the birds,
I would sing to them in praise of their wings,
I would urge them to fly off in all directions
at once, over the trees and the hills and
the lustful bodies of small animals. And this
is how it was this morning, when—after

making love in the large bed—we walked
through the Porta dei Cappuccini toward the
Eremo delle Carceri, where Saint Francis
is said to have blessed the birds, and past
the thousand-year-old oak, now supported
by steel bars, and watched the white doves
kiss atop the stone balustrade. And I looked
at my wife, and praised her body and my body
and all the bodies of this earth for what pleasure
they can give. And I bathed my eyes in salt,
as Saint Francis did, for the little love we find
and how we cling to it and how, once we find it,
we live constantly in dread of losing it, as
the Buddhists say. And I blessed this life
once more for what it has given me, and
for what it has failed to give me, and will
fail again tomorrow. And I held my wife
in these dust-driven arms and spoke to her
in this one language I know so well: the old oak
creaking in the blessed air, the pious fishes
singing in the stream, this all I know of Perfect Joy,
and all the white doves kissing in its name.

V

DAYS WE WOULD
RATHER KNOW

DAYS WE WOULD RATHER KNOW

There are days we would rather know
than these, as there is always, later,
a wife we would rather have married
than whom we did, in that severe nowness
time pushed, imperfectly, to then. Whether,
standing in the museum before Rembrandt's "Juno,"
we stand before beauty, or only before a consensus
about beauty, is a question that makes all beauty
suspect . . . and all marriages. Last night,
leaves circled the base of the ginkgo as if
the sun had shattered during the night
into a million gold coins no one had the sense
to claim. And now, there are days we would
rather know than these, days when to stand
before beauty and before "Juno" are, convincingly,
the same, days when the shattered sunlight
seeps through the trees and the women we marry
stay interesting and beautiful both at once,
and their men. And though there are days
we would rather know than now, I am,
at heart, a scared and simple man. So I tighten
my arms around the woman I love, now
and imperfectly, stand before "Juno" whispering
beautiful beautiful until I believe it, and—
when I come home at night—I run out
into the day's pale dusk with my broom
and my dustpan, sweeping the coins from the base
of the ginkgo, something to keep for a better tomorrow:
days we would rather know that never come.

WISHES THAT COULD LAST
A LIFETIME

Now it is once again the cold morning
and I rise from my bed,
knowing it cannot go on like this,
but that it will go on like this, always:
Terrible, terrible beauty,
terrible beauty that endures
in the still air of night and slips
time and again between our fingers.
And in the harbor the boats sway,
they sway and they turn at their moorings,
restless children who are constantly leaving
and returning, only to leave again.
They slip in and out of the narrow channels,
as hope and the thousand wishes slip
between this and the next life, scurrying
like ants up hills whose end they'll never
live to see. Yet we hold to hope,
we hold to hope and the pale confusion
as the blind hold to their sticks and dogs
and the good words of their neighbors,
eloquent and purposeful. We hold to hope
like the old rip-cord we count to five
and pull time and time again, the sewage
we refine and drink from until our gills flap
in the mad wind and we fall to earth,
grateful and hyperventilating.
It can last forever: We can jump,
time after half-crazed time,
from the flames, we can dive

from the sinking ship and swim for shore.
It lasts and lasts. It goes on,
ephemeral as breath, wishful as all thinking.
Enough to last an entire lifetime.

THE HAPPY POEM

This is a poem against false piety and sadness.

It is a poem against the stupid equation of grief
and holiness, a poem that dares to laugh
at the wilted tulip and the burnt hyacinth.

This is a poem against the wide tie and the narrow tie,
a poem that refuses to turn into another elegy
for Crane or for Berryman or for Sexton or Plath.

This is the poem that was not at the Holocaust.
It is the poem of the happy Jew, against atonement
and low stools, against kosherness and the circumcised penis.

This is the poem that snuck into the Seder
to drink from Elijah's miserable wineglass.

This is a poem against false protestations of love
and avowals of grief, against false sincerity.
It is a poem for Simone de Beauvoir.

This is a poem against the uncirculating gift,
against the inactive sperm and the undropped egg.
It is a poem against blankets.

This is the poem that will love you madly for a night
or a weekend, but will never marry you.
And you will never forget it.

Most of all, this is a poem against self-imposed suffering.
It is a poem against all my own poems that fail to begin

with lines like: *For seven years, I have been here, loving your teeth.*

This is my poem. And it is your poem.
And it is not sorry about anything . . .

Not even this.

WHAT I BELIEVE

I believe there is no justice,
but that cottongrass and bunchberry
grow on the mountain.

I believe that a scorpion's sting
will kill a man,
but that his wife will remarry.

I believe that, the older we get,
the weaker the body,
but the stronger the soul.

I believe that if you roll over at night
in an empty bed,
the air consoles you.

I believe that no one is spared
the darkness,
and no one gets all of it.

I believe we all drown eventually
in a sea of our making,
but that the land belongs to someone else.

I believe in destiny.
And I believe in free will.

I believe that, when all
the clocks break,
time goes on without them.

And I believe that whatever
pulls us under,
will do so gently.

so as not to disturb anyone,
so as not to interfere
with what we believe in.

YOUNG BIRDS CRYING
LATE AT NIGHT

for Jane Cooper

At night you can hear them,
the small birds, as if they were calling
the names of their sisters and brothers
up at the moonlight, as if,
in the still, vintage air of night,
they had found their voices among the maples
and were crying their theories of the world
into the vast hypothesis of silence and darkness.

Wishes, Auden said, *are not horses,*
and I know it, as I watch the pulsating sky
devour the darkening fields, *wishes*
are not horses, but maybe wishes are birds:
the slim night-graffiti of their cries
above the vanishing earth, the hybrid harmonies
of their throats opening and closing
in the delicate nests, the flapping
of their impotent wings as the stars
ember and rise up
to light this palpitating world.

PRAISE

I roll from the bed mornings
knowing things fade
and renew as they will—

the persistence of mangroves
clinging for soil
to bits of driftwood,
the deliberate trek of mosses
from the Pleistocene
over stone.

Though I remember nothing
from past lives,
they convince me
of something so eternal
it defies memory,
a quiet so deep
even the murmur of thrushes
intrudes on it,
even love
usurps its tranquillity.

I am no longer a small boy:
I bear loss
with an epiphytic ease—
the air sustains me,
the dust,
the well-intentioned residues
of decay.

If I wake tonight

screaming,
remain still—
when morning comes,
all I will remember
are last night's stars . . .

what they disturb,
and what they rectify.

TODAY I AM ENVYING
THE GLORIOUS MEXICANS

Today I am envying the glorious Mexicans,
who are not afraid to sit by the highway
in the late afternoons, sipping tequila
and napping beneath their wide sombreros
beside the unambitious cactus. Today
I am envying the sweet *chaparita* who waits
for her lover's banjo in the drunken moonlight
and practices her fingers against the soft tortilla.
Today I am envying the green whiskers of God
that protrude through the ground and we call:
grass. Why, today is so lovely I even envy
the singing dead with their proximity to earth
and genitals of flowers. O Lord, I don't
want to die yet, I just want to emulate
the beautiful purposelessness of the flowers
and Mexicans! I want to be the perfect madman,
without remorse or metaphor, without reflection.
I want to sit here babbling to myself about lust
and disobedience until it kills me, so I can join
the chorus of the singing dead and the sleeping
Mexicans beside the wild chrysanthemums—
beside the rose, the sangría and the happy earth.

THIS IS IT

for John McNally

Ah, John, the world is cold
and we are in it. But
there is a place of no ice,
and sometimes I wake, look
through the windows of all my neighbors,
and they are rising from their beds
and drinking their coffee, and they
are leaving their houses to catch a bus
that will take them somewhere they have
no use for. But John, this is the world:
the street, the bus, the garbage,
and all the imperfect lovers who are
willing to love us despite our imperfections.
Not the heaven we dreamt of, but
the sweet sewage of something better
and worse that flows in the streets
and we have no choice but to call: home.
This is it. And if we say it, again
and again, we may yet believe it:
This is it. This is it. This is it.
The fragile envelope we call body,
the huge ambivalence of love, and the
dust we clean from our shelves and will
eventually turn to. *This is it,* friend:
the oak and the empty cup; the starling
and the half-burnt candle; the women
we are always leaving, and the wise women
who leave us before we turn to them in anger.
Let's say it again: *This is it.* This is
the white sky of November and the bird shit
that plops on our shoulders without warning

or reverence. This is the rain
and the old garments we have no use for,
the cruelty and wild wonder of not knowing
what we want. *This is it,* friend,
this is it. On this incalculable Thursday.
On the day of your birth. Happy Birthday.
This is it.

OVER OHIO

You can say what you want about the evils of technology
and the mimicry of birds: *I love it.* I love the sheer,
unexpurgated *hubris* of it, I love the beaten egg whites
of clouds hovering beneath me, this ephemeral Hamlet
of believing in man's grandeur. You can have all that
talk about the holiness of nature and the second Babylon.
You can stay shocked about the future all you want,
reminisce about the beauties of midwifery. I'll take this
anyday, this sweet imitation of Mars and Jupiter, this
sitting still at 600 mph like a jet-age fetus. I want to
go on looking at the moon for the rest of my life and seeing
footsteps. I want to keep flying, even for short distances,
like here between Columbus and Toledo on Air Wisconsin:
an Andean condor sailing over Ohio, above the factories,
above the dust and the highways and the miserable tires.

I AM SICK OF THE RICH

I am sick of the rich, the way
they are always searching
for the crack in the diamond.

I am sick of their unconvincing aphrodisia
and immaculate sweaters. Oh, I am sick
of their talk about inflation, the state

Of the arts. If only the papers would
ignore them. If only they would publish,
for a change, the guest list

At Abe Rabinski's in Sheepshead Bay
or Elbert McCoy's on Lenox Avenue
& 125th Street. I wish some starved eagle

Would come along and treat their jibs
like dead salmon. I wish all their funds
would raise themselves into the Atlantic.

I wish Robert Rauschenberg would take
back his bathtub and his floating goat.
If only the rich would suffer in silence,

As the poor do. If only they would live
like their fathers aboard the Titanic,
counting their emeralds on the ocean floor,

Chiseling their names into the eloquent
iceberg, complaining to no one in particular
of the darkness, the seaweed, the incredible poverty.

EPITHALAMIUM:
THE SINGLE LIGHT

for Dalton Delan and Stacey Berson

Maybe the bride-bed brings despair
For each an imagined image brings
And finds a real image there;
Yet the world ends when these two things
Though several, are a single light.

—W. B. YEATS, "Solomon and the Witch"

Just as *coitus* means, really, *to travel together,*
this trip, this movement away from the self
toward the self, this deep delirium of cross-
purposes and unsheathed desires is a journey too:
treacherous, magical, serious, yet also a kind
of substantial gaiety, a dance in which the partners
embrace, separate, and return again to a single
place, in which the other-image ventures out
toward its partner, whom it finds, alters, is
altered by and renews, as wind and sycamore
alter, rectify and renew each other; as the slow,
unalterable turning of the earth alters the galaxies
in some way beyond our seeing. But what are
journeys for, if not to change the very urge that
moves them to begin? And what's marriage if not
a going out that quiets as it moves? Oh, someone
will always be wishing you luck, friends, but luck's
just choice made lucky by repeat, the way a man
thrown overboard makes his own life lucky by
the same stroke time and time again. Why, if I
were God, I'd let these glasses fill again with wine
and luck as Zeus did for that old pair whose only wish
was that they might burn, flicker and go out again
as a single flame. I'd make you oak and linden as

they were and call the shade a silence in your name.
I'd name the birds' embellished song for yours:
a noble thing, this word that's given as the word (the vow)
was meant to be, this utterance that love alone makes true,
its single light still burning in your eyes.

DRINKS AND KISSES

It is not such a bad thing to settle for The Little Way, not the big
search for the big happiness but the sad little happiness of drinks and
kisses, a good little car and a warm deep thigh.
—WALKER PERCY, *The Moviegoer*

My mouth puddles with bourbon and the taste
of your thighs. O little joy, you flickering
star, what can I say to you that would suffice,
what small dance can we make among the pines
and wildflowers as an epigraph to holiness?

Once, I wanted the world to reduce itself
to innocence, gather in a small pile
at my feet, an elegy to limits and ineptitude.
But now I know we are only a deep breath
among the ferns, a dry mouth of piety
and desire. Desperate for happiness, I give in:

I swallow my drink and start my small car.
I pucker forth to kiss you among the dying trees.

LIGHT, AT THIRTY-TWO

It is the first thing God speaks of
when we meet Him, in the good book
of Genesis. And now, I think
I see it all in terms of light:

How, the other day at dusk
on Ossabaw Island, the marsh grass
was the color of the most beautiful hair
I had ever seen, or how—years ago
in the early-dawn light of Montrose Park—
I saw the most ravishing woman
in the world, only to find, hours later
over drinks in a dark bar, that it
wasn't she who was ravishing,
but the light: how it filtered
through the leaves of the magnolia
onto her cheeks, how it turned
her cotton dress to silk, her walk
to a *tour-jeté*.

And I understood, finally,
what my friend John meant,
twenty years ago, when he said: *Love
is keeping the lights on.* And I understood
why Matisse and Bonnard and Gauguin
and Cézanne all followed the light:
Because they knew all lovers are equal
in the dark, that light defines beauty
the way longing defines desire, that
everything depends on how light falls
on a seashell, a mouth . . . a broken bottle.

And now, I'd like to learn
to follow light wherever it leads me,
never again to say to a woman, *YOU
are beautiful,* but rather to whisper:
*Darling, the way light fell on your hair
this morning when we woke—God,
it was beautiful.* Because, if the light is right,
then the day and the body and the faint pleasures
waiting at the window . . . they too are right.
All things lovely there. As that first poet wrote,
in his first book of poems: *Let there be light.*

And there is.

FATHER

I hold a candle to your face:

In the light, the lines of you
are a latticework of loss—
three mothers, two wives,
an uncertain son
who thrashes about
in the brine of your eyes,
calling you *father, uncle* . . .

                              mother.

If all men want mothers,
what might we,
having none, want?
We could break
from that design—
take back the stolen rib
and the fig leaf, take back
the diaphanous heart,
take back the fluttering eyelids.

Father,
hermaphrodite,
mermaid and minotaur,

Read this
in any language:
*Lese dieses
in jede Sprache.*

Be water, Father,
be blood.

THE CURE

Not just my family, dear God,
but my times suffer from this,
and soon it is as if the whole world
were merely a single cell, dividing
and dividing like mitochondria
beneath a child's microscope. Oh,
it is not that the river wasn't beautiful
this morning as it ran between the willow
and the maple, or that the stars,
last night, did not reek of divinity.
No, it is not that the world lacks
for beauty, but that the body
could be so set against itself it
works backward, like a limpet
out of order, and now the phone
is ringing and my father is telling me
that my sister, too, has cancer,
and I can see the surgeon's knife
slicing beneath her breast the way,
as a child, I watched Mr. Metzger
the kosher butcher slice fat from
a cow's flank, and it suddenly seems
as if the breasts of all the women
I have ever known are being lopped off
without remorse, and who knows
but at this very moment my own body
is dividing against itself and I am only
a feigned Gulliver succumbing
to a ravenous Lilliput, oh, it is silly
to think I am immune to this, and yet
I do, and because I am trying to find

a cure for cancer, because I want to save
the breasts of all the beautiful women
from the cold knife of the surgeon
as it slices through my morning, through
the stars and the river, because of
this longing to stop things from dividing,
I write this poem.

WISHFUL THINKING

for Cynthia

I like to think that ours will be more than just another story
of failed love and the penumbras of desire. I like to think
that the moon that day was in whatever house the astrologists
would have it in for a kind of quiet, a trellis lust could climb
easily and then subside, resting against the sills and ledges,
giving way like shore to an occasional tenderness, coddling
the cold idiosyncrasies of impulse and weather that pound it
as it holds to its shape against the winds and duststorms of
temptation and longing. I like to think that some small canister
of hope and tranquillity washed ashore that day and we, in
the right place, found it. These are the things I imagine
all lovers wish for amid the hot commencements of love
and promises, their histories and failures washing ashore
like flotsam, their innards girthed against those architects
of misery, desire and restlessness, their hopes rising
against the air as it fondles the waves and frolics them skywards.
I like to think that, if the heart pauses awhile in a single place,
it finds a home somewhere, like a vagabond lured by fatigue
to an unlikely town and, with a sudden peacefulness, deciding
to stay there. I like to think these things because, whether
or not they reach fruition, they provide the heart with a kind
of solace, the way poetry does, or all forms of tenderness
that issue out amid the deserts of failed love and petulant desire.
I like to think them because, meditated on amid this pattern
of off-white and darkness, they lend themselves to a kind of
music, not unlike the music a dove makes as it circles the trees,
not unlike the sun and the earth and their orbital brothers,
the planets, as they chant to the heavens their longing for hope
and repetition amid orderly movement, not unlike the music
these humble wishes make with their cantata of willfulness

and good intentions, looking for some pleasant abstractions
amid our concretized lives, something tender and lovely to
defy the times with, quiet and palpable amid the flickers of flux
and the flames of longing: a bird rising over the ashes, a dream.

THE PUZZLE

for my father

In the old family photograph, they are all
dust now, except for you. Your last sister,
Erna, the one with the birthmark on her cheek
and the necklaces of sapphire, just this month
gone dustward. And Aunt Tina, the seamstress
with the smile as thin as a thread: *dust.* All
the smiling ones—even Clemmy, the one
with the incarnadined cheeks and sweet eyes
of burnt sienna, even Uncle Fred, the stamp collector
from Vienna with the meerschaum pipes—all
dust now. They are all ambassadors from
that other country, just as I, whose blood
still runs hot through the throbbing capillaries,
who love the birds and the air and the fragrant
skin of my lovely wife, would be an ambassador
from this one. How strange it must be for you,
who are always telling me: *now I am the last one,*
to see them gathered here, all image and memory.
How it must make you think, constantly now, of
your own dying, that last piece in death's long puzzle
of jigsaw and reunion. Nights now, the persistence
of breath your one desire, the slowed transistor
of your heart pumping the blood toward memory
and terror, you must hear them calling to you:
Come here. Come here, sweet brother. Come
sleep with us again. How cruel, to have been saved
for last, like the body's last spared cell against the
ravages of cancer, like the last resident of Minsk
during the pogroms. And yet *life* is what we want,
above everything—Just one more sighting of the
chestnut-collared longspur, just one more night of

listening to the feathers make love inside the pillow,
just one more afternoon of *La Forza del Destino*
on the radio. O Father, clutched piece of the puzzle,
all is forgiven! And I, who am still blood and desire
and the wild laughter of afternoon, I hold this piece
of you in my hand, wanting to hide it from whoever
is playing, wanting to abort this long puzzle of dyings,
running through the woods, loving you, urging the gods
to speak your name quietly into their strange completeness.

CHEERS

But the concept of health is rooted in the concept of wholeness. To be healthy is to be whole. The word health belongs to a family of words, a listing of which will suggest how far the consideration of health must carry us: *heal, whole, wholesome, hale, hallow, holy.*

—WENDELL BERRY, *The Body and the Earth*

Imagine drinking to the health
of someone besides yourself: With your whole
heart, you hope your words will heal
whatever wounds the bright and hallowed
earth has brought him: hailstones
or pestilence, some small measure of holiness

and sanctity, the sacrament of breath. Wholly
human, you'd give of your own health
to help him, no matter where he hails
from, whether he was a Holy
Roller or an emissary from some hallowed
township you'd never heard of. His heels

click in the still air and, healed
of too much love for your own life, you're wholly
human for at least a moment: hallowed
be *his* name. But it's not healthy,
this other-love, your times say: the whole
of your energies should be one long Hail

Mary toward your own salvation, haling
your own self out of a private darkness to what heals
you. But how, you wonder, can the whole
self be occupied with the self—What holiness
is there in that? And to whose health
could a cup drunk in the dark, however hallowed,

possibly inure? It would be a hollow
ritual, no matter where your friend might hail
from. Nor would a single soul's health
be improved by it. And whose business is holiness
anyway? Socrates said: *Physician, heal
thyself,* and yet it seems there's a hole

somewhere in that thinking: the whole
of our lives now suffers from it. Say hello
to someone besides yourself and who knows how wholly
good you might yet become: hale,
healthy, and happy beyond all seeming. Healed
of your own significance, the health

you drink to might yet be your own: you a hale, wholesome
fellow grown whole from the weak heel of your own making,
hallowed the names of your loved ones, in sickness and in health.

DAYENU

Dayenu (Hebrew): "it would have been enough." The refrain from a Passover lit-
any thanking God for the blessings bestowed upon the Jews during their forty-
year wanderings in the desert following the flight from Egypt.

Had he rescued the nightingales from the floods
and not shrouded the planets in secrecy,

Dayenu.

Had he shrouded the planets in mystery
but not enticed us with the light that shines from them,

Dayenu.

Had he enticed us with the light that shines from the planets
but not created the pasqueflower to console us in winter,

Dayenu.

Had he created the pasqueflower to comfort us in our longing
but not allowed us to sleep by the river,

Dayenu.

Had he allowed us to dream on the banks of the river
but not given us the nostrils with which to remember,

Dayenu.

Had he provided us with the olfactory joy of memory
but not made the breasts of women so terribly beautiful,

Dayenu.

Had he made the breasts of women delicate as raspberries
but not given us the lips with which to honor them,

Dayenu.

Had he created the mouth as a tribute to women
but not allowed us to prosper in loneliness,

Dayenu.

Had he allowed us to thrive in our loneliness
but not created the darkness to sleep with us,

Dayenu.

Had he fashioned the darkness for our spouses
but not provided us with dust for a mirror,

Dayenu.

Had he given us the dust as our heritage
but not taught the earthworm to weave in our ruins,

Dayenu.

Had he instructed the earthworm to help us breathe again
but not permitted us to rise and praise the morning,

Dayenu.

Had he allowed us to rise into the white arms of emptiness
but not to rely on our fathers for mercy,

Dayenu.

Had he asked us to rely on the benevolence of misers
but not lifted the mist to uncover the dandelions,

Dayenu.

Had he lifted the mist to reveal the dandelion
but not taught us to sing without speaking,

Dayenu.

Had he allowed us to sing without movement
but not created the silence in which to practice our music,

Dayenu.

Oh, it would have been enough, Lord
Dayenu, Dayenu.

And for years.

ACKNOWLEDGMENTS

Knowing ourselves both best and least of all, we tend to be either too eager or too reluctant to believe in our own gifts, however large or meager they may be. These people, friends and poets—sometimes both—believed in mine: Dalton Delan, Jody Bolz, Charles Fishman, Irene Rouse, Grace Schulman, Robert Gilson, Richard Dunham, Jerome Bernstein, Maxine Kumin, Coco Gordon, Phyllis Wender, Anthony Hecht, and, above all, Howard Nemerov, whose music, intelligence, and integrity have been a continuing inspiration to me. To each of them, this book owes a great debt, lingering and unrepayable.

Special thanks to Amanda Vaill, for her careful and attentive reading of the manuscript and helpful suggestions, and to Stacy Schiff, more pearl than pill than she can ever imagine. Thanks also to my good friend Michael Collier for his valuable and generous reading of this manuscript, and to Morrie Warshawski, from whose own poem the last line of "Dayenu" was, ever respectfully, stolen.

The author wishes to thank the following magazines and periodicals, in which poems included in this volume first appeared. Some of the poems have been slightly revised since their original publication.

The American Scholar: "Waving Good-Bye to My Father" and "Squid"; *Aspen Journal for the Arts:* "Some Nights at Thirty"; *Associated Writing Programs Newsletter:* "Night Baseball"; *Bennington Review:* "The Music of Whatever," "The Happy Poem," "Jungians & Freudians at the Joseph Campbell Lecture," "Ordinary/Extraordinary," and "Who Will Live in Our Houses When We Die?"; *The Devil's Millhopper:* "A Photograph of Giacometti" and "Loss"; *Georgia Review:* "Today I Am Envying the Glorious Mexicans"; *Kansas Quarterly:* "October Sestina: The Shadows"; *Kayak:* "What I Believe" and "Wishes That Could Last a Lifetime"; *Long Pond Review:* "I Am Sick of the Rich"; *Louisville Review:* "Looking for Wildflowers in Bernheim Forest," "Poem, Against Hesitation," "Before a Storm, In September," "Twice-Born Matches," and "Drinks and Kisses"; *Missouri Review:* "The Woman Inside" and "Fish Fucking"; *The Nation:* "In Assisi," "Praise," and "Mushroom Hunting in Late August: Peterborough, N.H."; *The National Forum:* "The Elephants Dying" and "Dayenu"; *Nimrod:* "The Bitter Truth" and "The Cure"; *Ploughshares:* "Freudian Slip"; *Poet Lore:* "Watching *La Bohème* with My Father," "Poems by Someone Else," and "This Is It"; *Poetry:* "Cheers," "What Survives" (under the title "Life Goes On"), "The Flirtation," "Days We Would Rather Know," "The Disappointments of Childhood," and "Back from the Word-Processing Course, I Say to My Old Typewriter"; *Poetry Now:* "Melancholy"; *Prairie Schooner:* "Puer Aeternus," "Over Ohio," "Learning by Doing," "The Old Painter at the Violin," "Winter Light," and "The Earth Was Tepid and the Moon Was Dark"; *Southern Poetry Review:* "Last Supper"; *Tendril:* "A Man Lost by a River"; *Three Rivers Press:* "Blue" and "Juliek's Violin"; *Three Sisters:* "Leap Child"; *Virginia Quarterly Review:* "The Garden"; *Washingtonian Magazine:* "Christmas Eclogue: Washington, D.C."

"Fish Fucking" also appeared in the *Avron Prize Anthology,* Ted Hughes & Seamus Heaney, eds., Kilnhurst Publications, England, 1980.

"The Flirtation," "Squid," and "Waving Good-Bye to My Father" were reprinted in *The Anthology of Magazine Verse & Yearbook of American Poetry,* Alan Paton, ed., Monitor Book Co., 1980 and 1982.